KNOWLEDGE IS THE NEW MONEY
Making the Transition from College to Corporate or Career

Michael Askew

KNOWLEDGE IS THE NEW MONEY
Making the Transition from College to Corporate or Career

Michael Askew

Copyright © 2021 by Michael Askew

All rights reserved.

This book or any portion thereof may not be reproduced or used in any manner whatsoever without the express written permission of the author except for the use of brief quotations in a book review or scholarly journal.

Books may be ordered through booksellers.

ISBN 978-0-999-34771-3

Library of Congress Control Number: 2021905181

NuVision Publishing
PO Box 4455 | Wilmington, NC 28406
www.nuvisiondesigns.biz/publications

Printed in the United States of America.

DEDICATION

This book is dedicated to anybody who needs guidance and advice concerning how to make the transition from college to their career. Many people rarely think about transitioning into their career or if they are prepared for life after college until that awakening moment when they realized that they aren't ready for their first job after college. Being afraid and confused about making the transition from college to a job is something many young adults have secretly struggled with for many years.

The ***purpose of this book*** is to provide a blueprint for college students and graduates that will put them in position to achieve their goal of someday transitioning to their dream career. If you google the word competent, the definition will read *"having the necessary ability, knowledge, or skill to do something successfully"*. Now, google the word confidence and the definition will read *"the feeling or belief that one can rely on someone or something"*. In other words, *confidence* is when you believe you have what it takes to get the job done and being competent is when you actually have what it takes to get the job done. Many college students and graduates are realizing that they lack confidence, competence, or both. The goal of this book is to not only help you attain the confidence and competence that you need as you transition from **college to your career;** it is to inform and make you aware of what you don't know about transitioning into your career. College does a great job of preparing students to be analytical and to work hard for their career, but college does not prepare students in how to better be mentally prepared for success in their future career. College students shouldn't feel like they're transitioning from college to their career with a blindfold on; they should be confident that they know what to expect and how to be successful, regardless of what life throws at them post-graduation.

Table of Contents

Chapter 1: "I Made It To College...Now What??" 9

Chapter 2: Treat College As If It's Your Company
or Employer 13

Chapter 3: Test Drive Your Career Before You Live It
for the Rest of Your Life 21

Chapter 4: Companies Hire for Character
Skills Can Be Taught 29

Chapter 5: Learn The Culture of the Company ASAP 37

Chapter 6: Have A Clear Understanding
of Your Boss's Expectations 41

Chapter 7: Your Employer Invested In You-Give Them
A High Return On Their Investment 47

Chapter 8: Companies Want New, Fresh and Innovative Ideas-
That's Why They Hired You 55

Chapter 9: What Will People Say About You
When You Leave the Company? 59

Chapter 10: Find Somebody You Admire and Duplicate
Their Success By Being A Mentee 63

Chapter 11: Unrealistic Dreams Are the Key to Success 69

Chapter 12: A Sense Of Entitlement Is A Cancerous
Mentality to Have 73

Chapter 13: Your Goals and Actions Are Too Small 77

Chapter 14: Shameless Persistence Propels You
from Good to Great 83

Chapter 15: You Have Everything You Need
to Get Anything You Want 89

Chapter 1
"I Made It to College...Now What??"

It feels like yesterday when I was walking around the campus at North Carolina A&T State University while trying to convince myself I belonged there. It was my first time being out of Bertie County, North Carolina for an extended period of time. My mixed emotions of wanting to party with the rest of the freshmen conflicted with my homesickness, but I did my best to not let my homeboys notice that I missed home. Life after high school is similar to life after college in that you're entering a new chapter in your life where you need to have a different mindset to adapt to your new environment to be successful. In my book **"Knowledge Is the New Money: Making the Transition from High School to College,"** I talked about the opportunities and challenges that are associated with making the transition from high school to college. College students and young adults like yourself will find that the uncertainty and fear they felt as a freshman in college will also be present when they acquire their first job after college. You will be at a different stage in your life, but you will encounter familiar situations and emotions as you learn how to adjust to your current situation.

Begin with the End in Mind

Successful and results-driven people often make decisions based on what their life will look like one, five, or ten years from now. People with 4.0 GPAs accomplish their goals by studying hard, attending class regularly, and getting advice from people who are where they desire to be in life. Lawyers choose the appropriate major in undergrad and enroll in an accredited law school to give themselves the best opportunity to accomplish their goal. You need to take similar steps to reach your ultimate goal.

Unfortunately, many people didn't "get the memo" that they have to begin with their ultimate goal in mind to experience success in life. As a result, they find themselves wandering through life aimlessly while blaming the world for their failure or lack of success. It always worries me when I hear first- and second-year college students say that they're undecided about their major because this is a sign that they are not starting their college experience with a particular goal in mind. Not knowing what you want to major in is a sign that you don't know or care where you will be five or ten years from now.

Like many young people all over the world, I thought having the mindset of "I just want to be successful" was enough to help me get through college. I thought this mindset would be sufficient until I figured out what I wanted to do in life; boy, was I wrong. I wasn't one of those students who had an undecided major, but I was just as confused as the students who didn't know what they wanted their future to look like. I chose business management as my major only because I knew I wanted to be a businessman in the future. Not having a clear understanding of what I wanted to do for a living played a major role in why I didn't have a better reason for choosing my major.

Don't be like most college students. They spend thousands of dollars paying for school and many hours completing assignments just to realize during their last year that they don't like their major and would prefer doing something they'd enjoy for a living. This mistake and lack of preparation happens so often that it's almost considered normal to the college community. Nobody really talks about it because it's understood that the majority of people feel the exact same way.

How good would it feel to graduate college and walk into a career you've been dreaming about since your freshman year? In one of my classes during my last year of undergrad, I vividly remember looking to my left and hearing people talk about how they had no idea what they were going to do after they graduated. It was obvious that they cared more about not having to go to school any more than they cared about actually having a plan for how they'd make money once they crossed the stage. But the students on my right were a little different. Although they went through the same grueling four years as the students on my left, their post-college plans sounded more optimistic and calculated. Instead of having plans of chilling and being relieved that they didn't have to study for exams anymore, they were preparing to learn the challenging role of working for some of the largest companies in the US. Unlike the young adults on my left, the students on my right didn't worry about how they would make money after college. **Their biggest concern was if they should take the job offer in California for 80,000 a year or the one closer to home on the east coast for 50,000 a year.**

By the time I walked away from all the students, I realized that the students on my right had more options than those on my left. I also realized I was in the same position as the students on my left. After spending years in college trying to figure out who I was, what I wanted my future to look like, and how to make my dreams of being successful become my reality, I decided to be more like the students who were sitting to my right.

It's been said that college will be the best years of your life because you get to have tons of fun. The reason why most people say college will be the best time of your life is because they didn't put themselves in a position to have college-type fun even after they graduated. Life after college doesn't have to consist of going back home to live with your parents or working at a job you hate for the rest of your life. By planning for your future and starting with the end in mind, the best years of your life will be after college; the difference will be that you'll have more money to spend then.

Do you allow your current situation to dictate how you feel about your future? Many people get sidetracked from focusing on their goals because their emotions are wrapped around their current situation. After researching some of the most successful people in the world—such as Mark Cuban, Oprah Winfrey, Michael Jordan, and Steve Jobs—I realized they all had one thing in common: they all knew they would someday be successful, even when their current situation seemed to say the total opposite. Their confidence to keep going when nobody believed in them was a result of believing they would someday achieve life-changing success. As a college student, you have to keep your eyes on the prize. The company you want to own or work for after college should be all the motivation you need to endure the long hours of studying and the adversity you will experience along your journey.

Chapter 2

Treat College as if It's Your Company or Employer

I've never met a student who enjoyed learning something that wouldn't benefit them in the future. Think about all the times when you or your friends complained to each other, "Why do we even have to learn this stuff anyway? We're never going to use this in our career!"

> **The reason why it's important to have the desire to learn everything—even if it is something you can't relate to—is because you will come across many opportunities in your life that you could capitalize on if only you have been exposed to the right information.**

As a college student, I used to get annoyed and complain about having to get up in front of the class to present. Years of presenting during different situations in college appeared to be a waste of my time, but it actually gave me a competitive advantage when I got my first job after college. You never know what hand life will deal you, so you always have to be prepared and *use every experience as a moment to learn and improve.*

My manager got fired within the first three months of me working at Sam's Club Headquarters, my first corporate job. I noticed how everybody tried to act calmly, but it was obvious that the company was nervous about how they would continue performing well after letting go of someone who was very good at their job. Although I was new to the company and wasn't up to speed on how to do my current job, I was asked to take over the role of my previous manager while continuing my role, as well. I wasn't a stranger to hard work and pressure because college prepared me to perform well under pressure and while carrying a heavy workload. The only difference between college and my new role at Sam's Club Headquarters is that I was now responsible for managing $250 million worth of inventory, whereas in college I was just managing my GPA and my future. I will never forget the day I was informed I would have to present the Profit & Loss (P&L) data for my department in front of the top executives in the company. To say that I was scared and nervous would be an understatement. While trying to find a way to calm my nerves enough to present without collapsing on the floor in front of everybody, I began to think about the countless times I presented in college. The constructive criticism I received from my teachers and professors about my presentation skills raced to the front of my mind. The tricks and habits I used to calm my nerves and present well throughout college began to resurface. I remembered I used to memorize data and information enough to speak about it to the audience fluently and efficiently without letting them know I was nervous. I would add my own swag to my presentation to make the audience and myself comfortable. Once I arrived in the room to present in front of the executives, I noticed that the people who presented before me seemed nervous, unprofessional, and a little unprepared. When asked to present their findings, they would remain in their seat as they presented because it was more comfortable for them. The fact that I was the youngest of the group and the only minority who would be presenting inspired me to do my very best to meet and exceed the expectations and standards of my company.

When my name was called to present, I stood up and walked to the front of the room with enough **confidence to let them know I was prepared but with enough humility to show that I was grateful for the opportunity** to be there. To the surprise of everybody in the room, I did great! While I was driving home after work, I began to think about what the outcome of that

Presentation would have been if I didn't take my college presentations seriously. I thought about how taking college seriously and treating it like a business would not only result in good grades, but it would also prepare you for life afterward.

History often repeats itself. The students who prepare for presentations and other assignments in college will usually be prepared for opportunities after college. But the students who go through the motions of doing work only when they feel like it will do the same in the future. They won't have as many opportunities as the former group, and they won't even capitalize on the opportunities that will come their way.

Which Student are You?

If you're the student who doesn't take your future seriously enough to prepare and perform well now, this is your moment to change. People look at me as if I'm special or extra smart because I worked at the headquarters of Sam's Club and Belk, two of the largest public and private retailers in the world. But what they don't know is that I used to be the student who didn't take their future seriously. I told everybody I wanted to be successful, but my actions showed them I wanted to remain average. It took getting a 1.9 GPA and the threat of being kicked out of college to get my act together and become the best version of me. I was fortunate because there are many people who didn't bounce back from a slow start in college. Now is the opportunity to take your education and college experience seriously. Remember, every decision you make today is slowly but surely creating what your life will look like after college.

By treating college as if it's your own business, you will immediately become a responsible student who isn't satisfied with mediocre grades or results. As a business owner, you have to perform well today, or you won't be in business tomorrow. If you produce mediocre results for your employer, you may be one of the first to get laid off if the company needs to downsize. But by taking pride in your work and giving 120% in everything you do, your results will set you apart from other students, companies, and employees. What makes you different from the hundreds of students on your campus? Why should an employer hire you instead of another student with a higher GPA and more experience? Students typically don't think of the answers to these types of questions until they're in their third or fourth year of college, which is almost too late to answer them appropriately.

Let's face it, the main reason you're in school is not to get a degree; it's because you want to make a lot of money. The world is full of people who have multiple college degrees but continue to live paycheck to paycheck like those who never stepped a foot on a college campus. The reason why people get a college degree and continue to struggle financially is because they treated college like a hobby rather than a business that could put them in a position to make hundreds of thousands of dollars in their lifetime. You may not realize it, but every action you make now shapes your future.

Since I graduated from North Carolina A&T, a college that's known to have the best homecoming on earth, you can probably imagine the lifestyle I had in college. I partied hard, partied long, and partied from Thursday night through Sunday morning every weekend. I'm definitely not trying to be the fun police and tell you not to party because I believe having fun and partying helps relieve stress from the rigorous challenges of college. You just have to understand that **if you're going to party hard, you also have to be prepared to study even harder.** Find that balance in your life which allows you the time and energy to study and be prepared for all your classes but to also enjoy time with your friends. To be honest, partying feels so much better when you just made an A on a final exam. Unfortunately, the students who don't take their college experience seriously will party hard and long no matter if they made an F or an A.

Greatness Is a Choice, Not a Right

Everybody believes they deserve to be successful. Everybody believes they have the right to have the finer things in life and be chosen for the best opportunities. By looking at the face of a 5-year-old or even a 35-year-old, it would be obvious to see how they feel when they aren't chosen to be the winner of a game, accepted into the college of their choice, or are denied the opportunity to work at the company of their dreams. They believe they have the right to achieve a certain level of success, and anything below that is unacceptable. It's okay to desire greatness, but you have to understand that success won't be given to you; you have to earn it. It's your right to want more in life, but it's also your choice to do what it takes to obtain what you want.

College students often struggle during their first few years because they subconsciously believe they deserve to be successful, whether they have a strong work ethic or not. Years of being spoiled and given whatever they desired from family, friends, loved ones, and even high school teachers created the perception that life will hand over success on a silver platter, which is far from the truth. The moments when your high school teacher allowed you to retake a test because you started crying after you saw your grade made you believe you could always have your way if you could get people to feel sorry for you. **NEWS FLASH: having such a mentality will catch up with you in college, and especially after college.** I always thought life would work out for me because although I was never considered to be the smartest person in the room, I was always one of the most polite and well-mannered guys in the room. While growing up, I noticed that I often got my way simply because adults respected how I carried myself. Subconsciously, I began to use my politeness to get my way at home, at school, and in other areas of life.

You'd be surprised at how far being polite and saying "Yes, sir" and "No, ma'am" can get you.

I wasn't trying to deceive or trick people; I really thought life rewarded people by how they acted and how they treated others. College taught me that although being polite can open some doors for you, obtaining success and greatness can only be achieved by making the choice to work extremely hard to become the person you want to be and have what you want to have.

After having excellent attendance, sitting in the front row, and always behaving in my classes didn't result in passing grades, I realized I was doing something wrong. I immediately began to wonder if college was meant for me or if the professors liked me. By observing the students who made good grades and having conversations with professors, I realized my ability and choice to make good grades outweighed how much of a nice guy I was. When companies came to my college to recruit, they didn't care to know what I thought I deserved or how nice I was. Companies only wanted to know what my GPA was and if I had a history of producing great results. My first corporate job also gave me a taste of reality by showing me that people want results at the end of the day. I moved my family about 20 hours away from home for a job opportunity to work at the headquarters of the largest retailer in the world. My manager got fired while she was still training me, which meant I was next in line for taking over her duties and responsibilities. I struggled to handle the responsibility of taking over my manager's tasks because I had so much going on in my life. If being a first-time father and husband wasn't enough, the fact that we were hundreds of miles away from our hometown made our situation more complicated. I thought I was ready to handle this situation like a responsible adult, but subconsciously I expected my managers to be understanding of my situation, especially if I didn't perform up to the company's standard. Where did I get that mentality from? Who gave me the idea that success was deserved rather than earned? Although my situation wasn't easy, it was up to me to rise to the challenge and perform well. It was totally up to me to give myself a chance to be great by giving everything I had to be the best person I could be. The reason why most college students struggle with making a smooth transition from college to corporate America or their career is because they go into their first job thinking they deserve to be there, to make the amount of money they make, and to eventually get promoted to being the CEO someday. Just because you want to be successful and make a lot of money doesn't mean you deserve it or that it will be given to you on a silver platter. You don't get what you want in life simply because you want it; you get it based on who you are and how hard you're willing to work for it. The moment you realize nothing is given to you and that you have to work extremely hard for everything you want in life, the sooner you'll be living the type of lifestyle you always dreamed of.

Chapter 3

Test Drive Your Career
Before You Live It for the Rest of Your Life

      Would you purchase a new dessert before asking to sample it first? Would you purchase a car without asking to test drive it? Would you purchase a new pair of shoes without trying them on? Although most people would answer each of these questions with a firm "no," many people will actually choose a career without trying it out to see if they'll actually like it. Successful people often think three steps ahead of where they're going. It's not enough to want to be successful; you also have to prepare and plan for how you will obtain success. Like many college students, I struggled with understanding how important it is to test drive my career before I graduated. Since I struggled academically early on in college, it was difficult for me to get an internship and experience what my life would look like if I got a job relating to my current major. Internships are a great way to find out what type of job you would want after college, but you may never get the opportunity to intern anywhere if you don't take your education seriously enough to make the appropriate grades to qualify for the internship you want. Most companies require students to have a 3.0 average GPA. Maybe I would've tried a little harder to make good grades when I first enrolled in college if I realized that every grade I made helped to shape my future. The fact that my GPA was substantially lower than a 3.0 hindered me from test driving some of the best jobs you could imagine getting as a young adult. Earning an internship or volunteering in the career field that you're interested in, allows you to learn so much about employers, yourself, and life itself. You may think you want to work at the headquarters of one of the most popular companies in the world, but after experiencing an internship, you may have a change of heart. Changing your mind to pursue a different career doesn't mean you aren't smart enough to be successful in your current path; it just means that particular career isn't congruent with your gifts, passion, and purpose.

Nobody's born knowing what they want to do for the rest of their life. It takes time and experience to figure out who you are and how you want to make a living. I started working in retail during my second year of college so I could make extra money to pay for school and grab a bite to eat if I had any money left over. My original plan was to work a few months and then play college football. While working part time as a cashier, I realized this would be a good opportunity to get internship experience as a manager. So, I decided to forego football and prepare for my future by gaining work experience that would look good on my resume. In one year, I went from being a cashier to being a store manager intern. This was such an amazing experience because it showed me what my future would look like if I decided to go into retail management. Instead of always working on the register and interacting with customers, I would be in meetings with managers to examine the daily sales and create a strategy for the employees to increase their productivity. That internship was life-changing for me because it showed me what I didn't want to do for the rest of my life. As a young adult, I used to think being successful meant making a lot of money, but a retail internship showed me that **money without happiness can breed regret, bitterness, and misery.**

How cool would it be to have the option to pick and choose the career you'd like to have after college? Think about how great you'd feel if you volunteer or intern at a company for a summer and realize you can see yourself working there for the next 40 years. Nobody wants to work at a job that makes them dread going to work the next day. Find ways to get involved in the type of work you're majoring in or studying because you'll see whether you're on the right track. Many college students complain about being tired of school, but they find themselves being afraid of or dreading the day they graduate because they realize they may not want to be an accountant or work in a manufacturing facility for the next five to ten years, even if that is what they majored in.

Is Your GPA an Accurate Reflection of You?

Let me start out by saying that I don't think your GPA is always an accurate reflection of who you are as a student. That being said, I would probably examine your GPA if I was in charge of hiring you and other college students. Why would I look at a college student's GPA before I hired them being that I didn't have an impressive GPA myself? I don't believe GPAs tell everything about you, but they do provide a quick projection of who you could become. Some college students start off with a great GPA, but they let it slip as they get closer to graduating. Declining GPAs could be caused by many reasons, such as lack of focus, taking too many classes at one time, working too many hours, and not studying enough. Some college students start off with a horribly low GPA, but they improve it as they get closer to graduation. This may be the result of not taking college seriously at the beginning, learning how to study as you get older, maturing and learning how to manage your time, or realizing your GPA has a huge impact on the company that hires you after college. You also have students who never had an extremely low or high GPA. From their first year of college to graduation, they managed to maintain average grades. Although these students never had what people may consider a bad GPA, the fact that they consistently produced average results could mean they'll only do just enough to complete an assignment instead of going above and beyond what's been asked of them.

Whether you like it or not, people judge you based on the results you produce. I honestly felt like somebody had stolen my identity and pretended to be me in college once I understood how my GPA painted a picture of who I was and who I would be in the future. Companies wouldn't take me seriously because my GPA said that I didn't take school seriously and that I rarely exceeded the expectations set for me. Companies didn't care to hear how smart and intelligent I was; they just wanted to see if I consistently showed how smart I was based on my GPA. They could care less if I used to be a confused and immature young adult who was trying to figure out who I was and what college was all about during my first year. They simply wanted results. It's important for you to understand that results in your career will speak louder than any excuses or promises that will come out of your mouth.

A defining moment in my life is when I participated in my first career fair during my second year of college. I didn't know what to expect, but I was anxious to attend because I noticed all the students who appeared to be serious about their future made such a big deal about going. I found it odd that the students with mediocre grades didn't know or talk about the career fair, but the students with the good grades seemed to be well-informed and prepared for it. I still remember walking into the gym where the career fair was being held and trying to look as prepared as the other students who walked in before me. I walked from booth to booth paying little attention to the employers there but a lot of attention to the students who were talking with them. I noticed that the students who made the best impact on the employers were very good at selling themselves by explaining how they'd be an asset and bring value to the company. It immediately hit me that I didn't know how or if I would bring value to a company. After circling the career fair a few times, I decided to speak with my first potential candidate for a job opportunity. My bright smile and optimistic attitude slowly faded away as I struggled to explain how I would bring value to the company. Being that this was prior to my retail internship, I didn't have anything to show that I had experience in the type of position I was applying for. Every employer had three questions in common, regardless of the student's major. They wanted to know your GPA, your experience in that particular field, and how you would add value to their company.

As I slowly walked out of the gym with my head down, regretting that I even attended the career fair in the first place, an employer called me over to his booth and asked if I was looking for a job or an internship. The conversation went well until he asked me about my GPA. With little confidence and in a low voice, I shamefully informed him that I only had a 2.0 GPA because I started out so slow during my freshman year. He immediately interrupted me while I tried to complete my last sentence. He told me to lift my head up and always speak confidently, regardless of whether I had a 1.0 or a 4.0 GPA. He shared with me that **confidence is the first battle.** "If you have a low GPA, do not hide it," he said. "Put it on the table that you started out slow, but here is how I have improved, and this is how I plan to continue to improve." I walked out of that gym with the reality check I needed to complete the rest of my college experience with the end in mind. That career fair showed me that companies related a low GPA with being lazy, uncommitted, and undisciplined. I didn't believe my GPA was a true reflection of who I was, so I went on a journey to ensure my GPA reflected who I was from that day forward.

Unfortunately, students in middle and high school aren't informed about the importance of getting and maintaining a good GPA and how doing both can impact their life. People with low credit scores have a hard time getting a loan or buying things if they don't have cash because they don't qualify to buy things with credit. Sixteen- and seventeen-year-old teenagers can't party with the eighteen and up crowd at clubs because they don't meet the prerequisite of being at least eighteen years old. Life is full of situations where you have to meet some type of criteria in order to do certain things most people aren't qualified to do so. I had to learn the hard way that having a low GPA robbed me of the opportunity to attain scholarships, experience internships at well-known companies, and get numerous job offers from a plethora of companies post-graduation. I didn't understand the importance of producing an impressive GPA, so it's my duty to make sure you don't make the same mistake.

"Students with an Unimpressive GPA Need Jobs, too, Right?"

Having a low GPA during your last years of college while realizing you may not be able to find a job post-graduation can be a stressful, humiliating situation. Students who were responsible and informed enough to take their education seriously since the beginning of college deserve to be compensated by job offers in the city or state of their choice. But what about the students who started out slow at the beginning of college because they didn't understand the importance of education, how to be a successful college student, or how to balance their personal and academic lives? Many students graduate college and end up relocating back home to live with their parents, or they settle for low-paying jobs because they graduated college with an unimpressive GPA. I was almost one of those students until I heard my professor, Dr. Lester—who was also the assistant dean at the College of Business and Economics—speak to the soon-to-be-graduating seniors. She asked all the students who had a 3.5 GPA or higher to raise their hand and discuss the opportunities they had waiting for them after college. Needless to say, both of my hands stayed in my pockets. After my professor noticed that the majority of the class didn't raise their hands, she made a statement that changed my thinking forever. She said, "You know students with an unimpressive GPA also need jobs after college, right?" The room remained silent, but a loud celebration erupted in my heart and mind. I thought, "Finally! Somebody actually realizes how scared I am that I might not get a job after college because I struggled early on." The reason why I felt this way is because I've met and heard stories of many people who struggled to get acceptable grades in school and had a hard time finding employers who would hire them once they graduated college. The steps I took after speaking with Dr. Lester played a huge role in going from not getting attention from employers to being overwhelmed with so many opportunities to interview at the same companies that used to ignore me. *Here are the steps I took to increase my chances of getting a job offer before I graduated college:*

- I learned how to make good grades by observing and studying with the students who were where I wanted to be academically.
- I visited my professor's office often to get help with what I didn't understand and to get advice on how I could become the type of student employers want.
- I always kept my eyes and ears open to find ways to add to my resume, such as clubs, organizations, certificates, and volunteer work.
- I stayed in the back pocket of every person who worked in the career service. When they know you need a job, they'll refer you to employers when they visit the school.

If you're close to graduating and there's no way you can obtain a 3.0 or 4.0 GPA, there's still hope to land a great job and make a lot of money. You just have to be willing to work hard and find creative ways to stand out from the crowd of other students who are trying to convince employers to hire them. Work as if your life depended on it. When you think about it, your life and standard of living really do depend on if you get hired by a good company after college. I went to school with people who graduated and received jobs making $80,000 a year. I also went to school with people who graduated and got jobs making $35,000 a year. Both students went to the same school, and neither was smarter than the other. The only difference is that one of them took their education more seriously than the other and continued to find ways to become more attractive to employers. One student said that college wasn't worth it because they couldn't find a job afterward or they could barely pay their bills, but the other student reaped the fruits of their hard, consistent labor. They believed college is what you make it, and now they're doing great financially.

Which Student are You?
Which Student Would You Like to Be?

It doesn't matter where you are in life right now. All that matters is if you're willing to do what it takes to make your dream become a reality. You have every resource to be great in life, but you have to believe that it's possible for you to walk in greatness. I had to convince myself that I was capable of making good grades because I made bad and average grades for so long. Once I made up my mind that my future would be bright if I buckled down and worked hard, I became the student I wanted to be and always knew I could become. Students in their first and second year of college should understand how important their GPA is and use that motivation to be the best student they can be. But students with low GPAs who are in the final years of college should understand that it's not the end of the world and that they can still find ways to become a great student and an even better future employee.

Chapter 4

Companies Hire for Character
Skills Can Be Taught

One of the biggest misunderstandings I had about interviewing for jobs is that I used to think companies simply wanted to hire people with a 4.0 GPA and skills oozing out of their ears. Although companies value students with good grades and skills to match, they really aspire to hire people who possess good character. Employers understand that you could have all the talent in the world but won't make it if you would be toxic to the company and its culture. A student with good grades, experienced in a specific field, and good character, is a company's dream employee. I lost count of the number of interviews I had as a college student, but I remember that all the interview questions were similar. I had to answer scenario-and behavior-related questions because companies wanted to know if my answers were congruent with the type of employee they typically hire. You should experience as many mock interviews as possible because the more you interview for jobs, the better you will become at interviewing. My interview skills were horrible when I first started, but I improved exponentially by the time I interviewed and landed my first corporate job after graduation.

Don't Be Greedy,
but Know Your Worth—Negotiate

Do you know your worth? If you were an employer and had to hire a recent graduate who has similar skills, talents, and education as yourself, how much would you value that potential candidate? Would you pay them $30,000 a year for what they bring to the table, or would you pay them $60,000 a year? It is vital for every college student to know what they're worth to a company once they start searching for a job. The goal of every company is to hire the best employee for the least amount of money. Companies will dish out large amounts of money to acquire great talent, but a job candidate will need to show them they have unique skills that will maximize a company's potential. This doesn't mean companies won't spend big money on a recent college graduate; it simply means they want to get the highest level of production without having to pay a lot of money. Companies don't want to invest their money in a recent college graduate unless they're confident they'll be an asset to their business and that they'll receive a significant return on their investment.

This isn't an illegal or unethical practice; it's actually good business. Warren Buffett, one of the wealthiest people in the world, won't pay top dollar for certain stocks even if he believes they have a lot of potential. Warren has been called the richest man in the world for learning how to buy low and sell high efficiently. From a company's point of view, this is simply good business and smart investing. Hiring a sharp recent college graduate without paying top dollar for them can often result in a favorable return on investment for the company.

Okay, I know exactly what you're thinking: "Why should I care about how a million-dollar company can benefit by paying me a low or average salary when I can't even afford to pay rent?" I'm glad you asked. Once you stand in the employers' shoes and learn how they think, you'll become a better college student and the ideal employee, which will lead to you being compensated well.

Are You Irreplaceable or Can You Be Replaced by Anybody?

Average people do things just to say they did them instead

of actually attempting to give 120%. Successful people give it their all no matter what the situation is, and they get more satisfaction out of making a difference rather than by just going through the motions of finishing a task. Have you noticed that one of your friends despises losing even if they're playing a silly, pointless game, but another friend struggles to care about competing or winning even if they're faced with a serious situation?

> **Winners have a different mindset from others. They don't seek to win to gain publicity or attention. They aspire to win because the thought of losing or being labeled as average isn't allowed to settle in their minds.**

Winners win because the thought of losing or being average is more painful than their desire to win. They study long hours while their friends are partying because they don't want to get bad grades. They wake up at 5 a.m. to work out while their competition remains asleep because they want to be the best athlete on the basketball court, football field, or volleyball court. Winners put in so much work until they become irreplaceable to their team, organization, or company. Steve Jobs became irreplaceable to Apple, which is why they hired him back after they fired him. Apple realized they needed Steve more than he needed them.

People, companies, and organizations will make exceptions for you when you are irreplaceable. While working at Sam's Club Headquarters, I was mentored and trained by a very talented manager. She was a guru at manipulating an excel template, which is why people from every department admired her work. One day, I walked to my cubicle and realized she wasn't sitting across from me like usual. Nobody mentioned she was no longer with the company, but it became obvious after not seeing her for weeks that she'd been fired. I understood that companies let people go all the time for various reasons, which is why I wasn't surprised that she was no longer there. What did surprise me was that the company didn't realize how difficult it would be to replace her. This company made millions of dollars and attracted some of the brightest talent from all over the world, but nobody seemed to live up to my old manager's talent and skill set. The company lost money because everybody who stepped in to take her position was a downgrade. My previous manager didn't even have a college degree, but she was more irreplaceable than all the people in my department who had multiple degrees.

If you really want to be successful for a very long time, you have to **make yourself irreplaceable.** Find out what your job description consists of, then go above and beyond what's asked of you. The people who do enough just to get by will find themselves complaining about their low pay, being overlooked for raises or promotions, and being the first person to be laid off if the company needs to cut costs. Dr. Lester tried to warn me and my peers about the power of being irreplaceable, but I didn't comprehend how important it was. She said, "You need to differentiate yourself from the people who do not have a degree as well as the people who have a degree because they will be competing against you for a job." Having a degree doesn't necessarily mean you're the best person for the job. There are people searching for jobs who don't own a degree but will outwork you. They understand they can't use their degree as a means to get promotions, so they learn how to be innovative and persistent in everything they do. They understand that results speak louder than words and it's more valuable than a degree. Society puts so much emphasis on having a degree to the point that young people believe having a degree will guarantee them success and wealth. Unfortunately, this mindset is why young adults all over the world struggle to make a smooth transition from college into their career. Graduating from college and earning a degree is just the first battle you'll have to fight.

Remember, whenever one chapter is ending in your life, another one is beginning. Now that you've conquered the challenges of higher learning, it's time to find your way to success through the maze of your career.

Goodbye, College: Hello, Corporate America

College students' perception of life after graduation is a little confusing. During their second and third years of college, they'll be saying how they're so ready to finish school, but at the end of their last year, they'll begin to wonder if they're really ready to leave college and enter the real world. Many undergraduate students apply for and attend graduate school because they're afraid to enter corporate America or start a career after college. I wanted to attend graduate school because I wasn't satisfied with my undergraduate performance, and I wanted to prove to employers—as well as myself—that I was capable of producing exceptional work. During this time in my life, I remember overhearing students discuss how they really felt about school and life afterward. One particular young lady always complained about the graduate workload and how she didn't feel like doing it. One day, I looked at her with a confused look on my face and asked, "Do you like graduate school?" Without having to think hard about what I asked her, she immediately shouted, "No! I hate school! I'm only in graduate school because I'm afraid to get a corporate job." That's when it hit me that although students all over the world go to school to someday acquire a high-paying job, they're not confident they'll transition from college to their new career smoothly.

Although I'm now an entrepreneur, I learned a lot while I worked at my first corporate job after college. Saying I had a rocky transition from college to corporate would be an understatement. I had so many questions, but there either seemed to be very few answers or the answers were found after I made tons of mistakes. Since I had to learn how to adjust from college to corporate the hard way because there wasn't a blueprint for me to follow, I decided to create one for college students to follow in hopes of making their transition from college to corporate or their career a lot smoother than mine was.

Everything Is Negotiable, Even Your Starting Salary

The more you bring to the table, the more negotiating power you have. It doesn't matter what the situation is; your negotiating power comes from being an asset or by bringing value to the table in some way.

I was substantially underpaid at my first corporate job, and it was totally my fault because I didn't understand the power of negotiating. I was a customer service manager at a retail company when I heard I would become a father in nine months. I began to panic because although I'd been applying and interviewing with different companies to get a better-paying job, I didn't receive an offer from any of them. A week after my son was born, I finally got an offer to work at Sam's Club Headquarters. I was ecstatic because I knew I could provide for my family with this job. As I walked in a separate room from my wife and newborn son to speak with the recruiter and soak up the moment of getting my first offer from a corporate job post-college, I quickly noticed something seemed odd based on what she told me the company was willing to pay me. I was a bit confused because I had been with the company for years while I attended college full-time and got multiple degrees and certificates. My heart was excited to finally get a job after years of hard work in school but judging by the number of years I'd been with the company altogether, I expected to get a higher offer.

      After I accepted the offer and began working at the corporate office, I continued to be bothered by the fact that I was offered such a low starting salary. Part of me thought I was being greedy and unrealistic about what I would get paid after college, but a different part of me thought I should have asked for a higher salary. Unfortunately, I had no negotiating power. I did a pretty good job of hiding how I felt about my pay until my manager called me into his office during my second week on the job to speak with me. After I walked in his office and calmly shut the door behind me, I noticed he was staring at me like he expected me to start the conversation. He broke the silence by asking me how I was adjusting to my new position and if I had any questions or concerns. After I said all the right things and assured him that I was enjoying my first two weeks on the job, he continued to look at me as if he wanted to address an issue but would prefer if I brought it up. He finally addressed the elephant in the room by informing me that my starting salary and position should have been higher than what it was, but some of the employees—who were going to be my direct managers—weren't sure if I could live up to the task. So many thoughts went through my mind during and after this conversation—which I will share with you throughout this book—but the main thought was how every recent college graduate should know their worth so they can negotiate their salary accordingly. Perhaps the managers were correct in their assessment to offer me a low salary because they thought I couldn't live up to the job's demands, but what if they were wrong? The truth of the matter is that it isn't the company's priority or job to make sure you obtain a well-deserved salary. It's your responsibility to ensure you make enough money to provide for your family and that you reap the fruits of your labor for spending thousands of dollars to earn a degree.

      Now, I'm not advocating for recent graduates to be

unrealistic and greedy in what they expect to get paid straight out of college because I'm aware that the lack of experience many recent college graduates have is one reason why employers don't always pay college students top dollar. Expecting to get paid the same salary as the middle or senior manager of the company will make you seem greedy and unrealistic. Do some research to find out the average salary for the companies you're applying to by using websites such as Glassdoor or even Google. Having a clear understanding of what the average salary is for a marketing executive will give you an idea of what companies may offer you and how much you should ask for if they offer you a low salary.

So, there are **two steps** to getting the salary you want after you graduate. The *first* is to get education and experience to help you land your desired job and salary. The *second* is to research to find out the pay scale for certain fields and positions within companies. Following these two steps will put you on track to achieving your post-graduation goals.

Chapter 5

Learn the Culture of the Company ASAP

Isn't it embarrassing to see somebody walk out the bathroom with tissue stuck to the bottom of their shoe and everybody notices but them? We've all been in situations where we didn't have valuable information that everybody around us just happened to know. Needless to say, that's not a good feeling. Being interviewed or working for a company without researching and learning about its culture will make the transition from college to corporate more difficult than it has to be.

For some strange reason, I pictured every corporate job to be similar to the ones I'd seen on TV or in movies. Although I found out my perception of corporate America was totally wrong, I didn't understand the importance of adjusting to the actual culture until my actions and thinking began to clash with the culture of my first corporate job at Sam's Club Headquarters. Doing your due diligence to learn about and adapt to the culture of a company could be the difference between you being hired or passed over for a job.

What Does It Mean to Fit the Culture of a Company?

The tricky part about fitting a company's culture is that each one is different. You may fit your previous company's culture just fine, but you could be an absolute misfit at your next job. One of the reasons why it's difficult to guarantee you'll always fit a company's culture is that you can't measure or calculate it. An employer can choose numerous reasons why they feel like you don't fit their culture. You may be too loud and talkative in one culture, but you could be too shy and reserved in a different one. A supervisor at my first corporate job once told me a story of how it took him getting embarrassed at a company Christmas party before he understood the importance of learning a company's culture. He was invited to his first holiday party with a new company, so he decided to bring a couple bottles of wine because everybody brought alcoholic beverages at the parties he went to at his previous jobs. As soon as he got to the party, somebody escorted him to a private room and told him he would have to take the drinks back to his vehicle or leave the party. He was humiliated, embarrassed, distraught, and any other word that would explain the feeling of wanting to turn back time and act as if that event never happened. He explained to me that bringing drinks to parties and the office was normal at his previous company, but the culture of his new job was totally different than his old one. The previous company's culture consisted of working hard and playing hard, but the culture of his new company consisted of working hard and playing conservatively.

I didn't realize every culture is different until I left my first corporate job to relocate back home to North Carolina. I had a meeting with a company that sold tobacco products, and I was very excited because I knew that if I got that job, I'd have work once I settled in North Carolina. As soon as I opened the door to that company, I got hit by the strong smell of cigarette smoke, which made me start coughing and wiping my eyes. While I was having a meeting with the HR manager and recruiter in the lobby, they told me their building was always filled with smoke because the employees could smoke whenever they wanted. I was speechless. The interior walls and ceiling were originally white, but now they were a tannish, creamy color due to years of tobacco smoke settling onto them. As I headed home, I came to the conclusion that knowing, understanding, and feeling comfortable at a company is more important than any salary I could get.

I got the opportunity to work at my second corporate job shortly after relocating back to the Charlotte, North Carolina area. I figured the culture at my new job would be different from my previous one, but I didn't know how. From the moment I walked in the building to be interviewed, I noticed that this company's culture was less conservative than at Sam's Club, but I didn't know if that was a good thing. One day while I was working, I heard two employees talking to each other while dropping "F bombs" in their conversation as if it were routine. After I looked around and realized I was the only person that seemed to be surprised they were using that type of language in a business setting, it hit me that this culture was definitely different than what I expected.

It's vital to grasp a company's culture quickly by observing and paying attention to everything. From the moment you arrive in the parking lot for your interview, you should be prepared to take mental notes of what to do and what not to do once you start working there.

Chapter 6

Have a Clear Understanding of Your Boss's Expectations

It doesn't matter how well you know somebody. Sometimes you may buy something you're sure your close friend will love just to find out they hate it. "But…I thought you'd like this gift because you seemed to like similar gifts in the past" might be the answer you give to justify your decision. Your family, friends, or college professors may have forgiven you for things like that, but that won't fly in corporate America.

Have you ever heard people say that "Time is money"? Well, in corporate America, time actually is a lot of money. The longer it takes to finish a project, the more it costs the company. When you, your colleagues, or managers have to go back and fix a mistake you made, it costs money. Completing projects for your manager that don't meet their expectations not only causes your department to suffer, but it also causes the whole company to suffer, as well.

I believe one of the reasons I made many mistakes in corporate America was so you could learn from them. Or maybe I was just a horrible employee. Regardless, I just hope you can learn from my mistakes.

My peers and managers had to go back and fix many mistakes I made while I was working at Sam's Club because I was oblivious to what my boss's expectations were. I don't believe my first boss tried to set me up or hurt my performance by not telling me exactly what she expected of me and my department. I worked in an extremely tough department that managed and controlled millions of company dollars, and she understood how much pressure I would've felt if she put too much on me too soon. So, my manager's plan was to bring me on slowly so I wouldn't get overwhelmed. The manager I reported to directly was in charge of completing the difficult jobs until she trained me to take on a heavier workload. This appeared to be a great idea until she got fired, which put me in charge of managing a $250 million department.

Having to step up and take over someone else's responsibilities happens all the time in corporate America. On one hand, it's a scary thought, but on the other hand, it actually gives you an opportunity to show your employer what you can do. Unfortunately, I wasn't ready to shine once I got the opportunity to perform. Since my manager was in charge of running the show, I didn't see it as a priority to make sure I knew exactly what my boss's expectations were. I wasn't always 100% focused when executives or top-level managers would speak with my manager because I didn't think the information that they were giving her was meant for me. It wasn't until my manager got fired and I was expected to perform that I realized I should've had a clear understanding of my boss's expectations from day one.

Create Ways to Remember Your Goals

School and college consisted of memorizing tons of information and trying to remember everything on test day. Corporate America is totally different. Although you'll be asked to learn tons of information like you had to in college, you won't be asked to memorize most of it. Your employer won't care if you memorize the answer to the problem; they just want you to have or be able to find the answer.

If you were to walk into a corporate office right now, you would see sticky pads and calendars inside the cubicles to remind employees about certain events or projects. Now read really carefully because I'm about to share with you the best way to remember your goals and boss's expectations. Are you ready? The best way is to use a notebook and a pen. I know you were probably ready for me to inform you about some innovative technology or corporate secret you could use, but an old-fashioned notebook and pen or sticky notes will do the trick just fine. I couldn't contribute a lot during the meetings when I first started working because I didn't know enough, so I just took notes and asked a plethora of questions. Once you sign on the dotted line to work for a company, you're agreeing to approach your job as if it's your own business. You should want to learn as much about your position as possible by writing down everything and creating reminders around your sitting area to motivate you to hit your goals daily. If your company goal is to have a 95% rate on inventory in every store in your division, you should write "95%" right above your computer so you see it when you sit down at your cubicle.

It's extremely difficult to be on the same page with your boss and peers if you don't have a clear understanding of the company's objective and goals. How can you focus on having a 95% inventory rating when you don't even know what the goal is for your department? Adjusting to corporate America can be challenging because you're learning to think differently than you did in college, and you're also learning so much at once. People often feel as if corporate America is not for them, so they quit or get fired before they even get the hang of it. Although corporate America may not be for everybody, many people would perform much better if they had a system or plan to transition into that environment effectively and efficiently. Although I like to write down my goals because I sometimes like to do things the old-fashioned way, many people find it more convenient to use calendars on their computer or phone to remind them about certain goals or events. You may create ways of remembering your goals that are different from your colleagues, but you have to do whatever's best for you.

Knowledge Is the New Money
Making the Transition from College to Corporate or Career

Getting in the habit of taking notes and having a clear understanding of your boss's expectations can help you create better results and save you from possibly getting in trouble. Remember the times when your teacher graded your assignments wrong by mistake? When you approached them about a problem they marked incorrectly, they gladly gave you credit and changed your grade. Just like your teachers and professors can make mistakes because they're human, your supervisors and colleagues can make mistakes, as well.

What would you do if your boss told you to complete a project a certain way, but when you finished and turned it in, they tell you they wanted you to approach the project differently? It won't do you any good to inform them how wrong they are and how right you are unless you have some type of proof. One of the reasons why you should write down your boss's expectations is for proof just in case you need it in the future. Unfortunately, I had to learn the hard way that I should take notes and keep every document that was given to me, even if it was an email.

After my manager got fired from her job, it felt like everybody in my department was drinking water from a fire hydrant by trying to learn all the information she took with her when she left the job. It went from a smooth-running department to a chaotic, every-man-for-himself department. One day, my new manager called me into his office for our quarterly one-on-one meeting. The smile I had on my face when I first entered the room quickly disappeared as I realized he was writing me up for not performing at the company's standard. I obviously wasn't happy because nobody enjoys being disciplined for not doing their job, but it blew my mind that I was being written up. As my manager began to tell me all the reasons why I was getting written up, I suddenly realized that many of them weren't true and that someone else was to blame for some of the issues, but I couldn't prove it. At that very moment in that small room, he was able to blame me for anything he wanted, and I didn't have any other choice but to accept the blame because I didn't have any proof to say otherwise. It doesn't matter if the manager was wrong or right; at the end of the day, I had to make sure I was able to cover my butt and have proof for everything I did.

    I remember vividly daydreaming and talking in class when the teacher would suddenly ask me a tough question that caused me to look like a deer caught in headlights. Those were some of the most embarrassing moments I experienced in school, but I'm glad they happened to me because they forced me to pay attention. If you thought graduating from college would relieve you from being put on the spot and having to answer questions from your superior, you may want to think again. One of the reasons it's important to always know what the goal is for your department is, so you'll always be aware of how close or how far away you are from reaching your goal. Your boss could stop by your desk or call you into their office to ask you about the status of a project or your department at any time, and you'd be expected to come up with an answer that's better than "I don't know." The penalty for not being able to answer a question in college was only embarrassment, but the penalty for not answering a question in corporate America could result in embarrassment, loss of credibility, and being perceived as irresponsible.

    Most colleges don't warn students about the expectations that come with getting paid a high salary for working in corporate America, but I believe understanding how to transition from college to corporate properly is just as important as the wealth of information you learn in school. The fear of my boss stopping by my desk on her way to her office to ask me a specific question about my department motivated me to pay attention to my goals and learn my role inside and out. Not being able to answer questions about the progress of your project, department, division, or company says more about you than you may realize. You may think it's not a big deal that you couldn't answer a question, but your colleagues and supervisor often use your ability to answer a variety of questions about your job to determine how serious you are about it.

Chapter 7

Your Employer Invested in You— Give Them a High Return on Their Investment

It's easy to take something for granted when you don't have to pay for it or pay for it up front. Students often take their education for granted because although they take out loans to pay for school, they don't feel the immediate effects of performing badly or just well enough to get by. Unless you were fortunate enough to earn a full collegiate scholarship, you spent thousands of dollars hoping to get a college degree and ultimately a career that deals with your major. Some students think it's okay to quit or not give their all at times because they're the ones paying for their education; they don't think it hurts anyone else. This may be true to an extent, but this mindset is setting young adults up for failure once they arrive in corporate America. Once you enter your career, you'll realize that how you perform your job not only affects you but also your colleagues and employer. Nobody likes to feel as if they're just a number. Everybody wants to feel like they're special to the company that eventually hires them to spend the next 20 or 40 years in their career. Adding value to your employer and giving them a high return on their investment is a great way to ensure you won't be treated like a number or the average employee.

My favorite television show is "Shark Tank". This show consists of a group of people called "sharks" who invest in people and their ideas. It doesn't matter how nice the deal seekers may be or how much the sharks like them; the sharks only invest in people they believe will give them a high return on their investment. The sharks often use metrics such as previous sales and growth potential to make a final decision on whether they should invest thousands or millions of dollars into people and their businesses. Every company you interview and apply for are sharks, and you have to bring something to the table that will make them want to invest in you. Once a company decides to take a chance on you and pay you a salary—which will be more money than you've ever seen in your entire life—you have to show the employer that they just made the best investment of their life by bringing you on board.

Companies spend thousands of dollars going through the hiring process to choose the right candidates, and they also spend a lot of money firing and laying off employees. While reading an article from Forbes, I found out that companies have to consider employment taxes, cost of sickness, legal fees, red tape, and much more when they hire an employee. So, what should they do with the employees who don't make their department or company better? What should they do with the employees who do just enough to get by each day? These employees may not be losing the company money, but they aren't providing a return on the company's investment, either. These types of employees force companies to choose between retaining or firing average employees who waste their money and hiring employees who would actually be motivated to make them money. Companies that have the type of culture that allow for employees to do just enough to get by without adding significant value hurt themselves in the long run; this will ultimately be detrimental to the company's potential, bottom line, and employee morale.

Average Results Yield Average Recognition

It's important for recent college graduates to not fall into the trap of doing just enough to get by, especially when they see their colleagues have adopted that mindset after being with a company for years. What's interesting about employees who do the bare minimum is that they often complain about never getting recognition or a pay raise, and they find themselves being jealous of the employees who are making moves to get promoted and recognized. I recently heard a story about a professional football player being criticized because he made his son return a reward or trophy for coming in third place. The football player didn't want his son to get comfortable with the idea of receiving recognition just for participating in an event. When I first heard about this story, I thought the father was just trying to be macho and didn't want losing to be associated with anybody who shares his last name. But after I thought a little deeper, I realized the father was fighting to prevent his son from adopting the mindset of expecting something for doing the bare minimum.

Isn't it weird how society creates the perception early on in life that everybody should get an award for just trying and giving a little effort to win? As you get older, you realize that trying and giving mediocre effort will not be enough to succeed. Getting all your college credits will earn you a degree, but it doesn't guarantee you'll be qualified to work at some of the most well-known companies in the world. The students who complete all their credits, maintain a decent GPA and gain experience in their field of choice will have the best chance to work for the most well-known companies in the world. Now that you've closed the door on your collegiate years, it's time to open the right doors to help you excel during your professional years.

Say goodbye to the days when you expected a good grade from giving mediocre effort in college group assignments and say hello to giving 150% effort towards complex corporate projects. One of the reasons why my first corporate job paid me less than what I thought I deserved it because they wanted to see if I was willing to put forth above-average effort before I received an above-average salary. I didn't understand or agree with their decision initially, but I realized eventually that the position I thought I deserved would've been very tough for a recent college graduate to succeed in. Being successful in that position had very little to do with how smart I was as a person and more to do with whether a recent college grad could produce above-average results while solving complex problems with millions of dollars on the line.

Accelerate Your Learning Curve

The sooner you learn how to perform your job in a proficient manner, the sooner you'll be an asset to your company. On my first day at work, my manager told me that it usually takes three months to start catching on to how to perform my job, six months to work efficiently with no supervision, and one year to excel at my job to the point where I can make a difference and train others, as well. Of course, I took my manager's statement as a challenge to learn how to do my job a lot sooner than the time frame he told me. When I spoke with some of my friends who worked for other companies, they explained that they were expected to perform well within the first couple of months on the job and that their job security would be in jeopardy if they didn't. Regardless of what company you work for or the time frame your boss gives you to be up to speed on performing your job, you should aspire to learn every detail about your position, department, and company as soon as possible.

Although the first corporate company I worked for told me I wouldn't be expected to perform with minimal mistakes until the six-month or one-year mark, they actually needed me to perform at the three-month mark when the manager who was training me got fired from the company. I wasn't ready to take over my previous manager's duties because I had the wrong mindset. Since I was told it usually takes most people six months to work at full speed in their new role, I immediately erased the sense of urgency to accelerate my learning curve, especially when I realized my job was pretty difficult. If I struggled with comprehending how to do my job on week two, I didn't panic because I was told most people struggled until the third month; I'd substitute thoughts of trying harder with thoughts like, "Well, they'll understand if I don't perform up to their standards because most people don't perform well until the third month."

Companies are put in the awkward position of trying not to put too much pressure on new employees to perform at a high level, even though thousands of dollars can be made or loss by their results and performance. Some supervisors will use a stern, blunt approach to inform employees about the seriousness of learning their position as soon as possible, but other supervisors may use a soft approach because they realize the added pressure on new employees can affect their performance in a negative way. As a recent or soon-to-be college graduate, you should approach your new corporate or career position with thoughts of accelerating your learning curve so you can be an asset to the company sooner rather than later.

Want to Make a Name for Yourself as a New Employee? Master Your Job While Cross-Training at the Same Time.

I would have saved myself, my supervisors, and my company many days of stress and headaches if only I understood the importance of mastering my job ASAP while cross-training simultaneously. Okay, let's just start off by talking about the importance of mastering your job before you think about cross-training, which simply means to practice training for another role or skill.

The beauty about working with other people is that everybody's job somehow has an impact on everyone else's in one way or another. The unfortunate part about working with other people is that if one person doesn't do their job, it can cause the rest of the colleagues to have to do more work or receive mediocre results. The reason why I'm qualified to speak on this topic is because I've been the employee who hated to work with certain people since I knew I'd have to pick up their slack by working harder. However, I've also been the employee who slowed down progress within my department because I wasn't performing my job efficiently and effectively. It sucks to be in either of those positions, but it really sucks to be the colleague who drops the ball and doesn't do the job you're getting paid to do. From the moment you sit at your desk or cubicle for the first time, your mission is to be a sponge and soak up every ounce of information you're given while keeping your ears open to the information given to the people around you.

Don't be intimidated by the fact that most of what you hear people say will sound like a foreign language to you. The way you talk in code or slang when you're around your close friends will be similar to how everybody at the company talks to each other. This part of being a new employee can be very intimidating; it's difficult enough not knowing how to perform your job, but not knowing what people are talking about while you're clueless about how to perform can make you feel like you don't belong. Before you grab your jacket and belongings to leave the building with no intention of returning, just remember that everybody experiences the same feeling of uncertainty, fear, and not belonging when they get their first job after college. The key to overcoming those feelings is to persevere through the tough times by asking a plethora of questions and always giving 110% in all you do.

Learn everything about your department, company, and job like the back of your hand.

I'm not a smoker, and I never had the desire to start smoking even when it seemed like all the youth and young adults thought it was the next best thing since sliced bread. I'm not sure why smoking never intrigued me; maybe it was because most people I knew who smoked ended up becoming addicted to it at some point. So, you can only imagine how confused and lost I felt during my first corporate job at Sam's Club when I was put in charge of ensuring that stores all across the U.S. stayed stocked with tobacco products. I thought my job would only consist of learning how to order products and monitoring the inventory for stores, but I was wrong. The people who were really good at their job knew everything they needed to know about the tobacco products that Sam's Club sold. I struggled early on at my first corporate job because I had a difficult time separating my feelings of not liking tobacco products and never being a smoker from my reality of needing to learn everything possible about tobacco products so I could accelerate my learning curve and excel at my position. The difference between average people and successful people is that successful people do what they don't want to do because it moves them closer to their ultimate goal. If I wanted to stand out, get promoted, and move up the corporate ladder, I would have to learn everything about tobacco products as if I were a smoker so I could maximize the potential of my department and the company. Unless the company is asking you to do something that's unethical or goes against your morals, be prepared to learn about and do things you wouldn't normally do on your personal time.

Chapter 8

Companies Want New, Fresh, & Innovative Ideas—That's Why They Hired You

Although companies look to hire people who will fit their culture, they also look to hire people who will think outside the box and bring new ideas to the table. Recent college graduates have that advantage because they don't have years of work experience to fall back on. Most companies encourage new hires to speak up and think of new ideas for projects, but recent college graduates usually prefer to take the back seat to a colleague who's been with the company longer than them. Recent college graduates need to understand that there's no such thing as remaining the same. Either you're improving or you're regressing. Companies hire college graduates because they're hoping they'll help improve their company by bringing something different to the table. Recent college graduates usually turn out similar to the employee who train them, or they turn out to be like the other employees at the company, which could be either beneficial or detrimental. If a company has innovative, hard-working employees, new hires imitating them could be beneficial in the long run, but if the company has traditional-thinking, just-do-enough-to-get-the-job-done employees, new hires learning from them would be detrimental.

Meetings Are Your Time to Shine—Show Everybody What You're Made Of

I try to be careful when I talk about how college benefits people but also doesn't prepare them for certain situations in life because I'm not against pursuing higher education. But there is a perception among youth and parents all over the world that assumes that attending college will give you everything you'll need to be

Knowledge Is the New Money
Making the Transition from College to Corporate or Career

successful in life after you graduate. Contrary to what professors, teachers, and your parents have told you about college, there are a few things you will have to learn once you leave college. In fact, I was actually shocked to witness how college didn't prepare me for certain realities of corporate America. Before I graduated, I had actually spoken with people who were in their career, and they never talked about how much different corporate America is from college. After enduring the growing pains of not being fully prepared for a *career after college,* I realized many people aren't prepared for life after college. But recent and not-so-recent college graduates rarely discuss their growing pains with up-and-coming graduates, which leads soon-to-be graduates to believe they'll be ready to make a smooth transition into their career after college.

The college experience really helped me during the times I had to speak in corporate meetings. All those days when you used to shake in your dress suit and shoes because you were extremely nervous before you opened your mouth during a presentation are the moments you'll need to tap into and remember when you get a job after college. The four years I spent speaking in front of the class while explaining my PowerPoint actually gave me confidence to speak in front of my colleagues. Although college prepared me to present and speak in front of people, it didn't prepare me to bring value to meetings in corporate America. Speaking up and allowing your voice to be heard in the corporate world is important, but that doesn't mean you should speak if you don't have anything valuable to say. Have you ever witnessed a person opening their mouth and saying a lot of words without adding value to the conversation? They basically wanted to talk just to be included in the conversation regardless of whether they had anything important to add. Don't be that person when you attend meetings at your new job.

Who else would be better at warning you about the embarrassment and shame that comes with not adding any value to a meeting than a person who has experienced such unforgettable moments? I was completely terrified to attend corporate meetings because I had a hard time trying to figure out what I should say and when I should say it. The business lingo, acronyms, and inside jokes were all foreign to me. My manager and coworkers expected me to contribute and have valuable input during the meetings, but I didn't know how. My goal is to provide you with the confidence and competence you'll need to be an asset at company meetings. Confidence is the belief you have about yourself concerning how you'll perform; competence is your ability to actually perform well. You'll need both to experience success during and after college.

One of the best ways to learn how to add value to a meeting is to be thrown into the fire of taking on more responsibility. People have a natural tendency to relax and give less effort when they have less work to do or when they don't have to be held accountable for certain things. I struggled in meetings when I thought new employees didn't have to immediately bring value to meetings until my manager got fired and I had to show up with vital solutions at every meeting. This was a scary moment for me, but it was the best thing that could've happened. Being forced to take on more responsibility made me learn every detail that had an impact on my department and the business as a whole. It became impossible to walk into a meeting without being prepared because I was now responsible for millions of dollars and all my colleagues depended on me to have solutions for problems or potential problems that could affect the company. After my direct manager got fired, a higher-level manager approached me and said, "Now it's your time to shine and show everybody what you can do." This is when it hit me that I was no longer in college and that I had to make decisions that would affect the company's bottom line.

The 20+ years of schooling you received from kindergarten through college rewarded you by giving you grades for your hard work. If you didn't do your homework or if you made a bad grade on your test, it had more of a negative impact on you than it had on the teacher and the school. Everything changes once you graduate college. When you don't perform well at your job, it hurts everybody. Being that the company is actually paying you to perform at a high level, they'll expect more from you than what your professor did. One way to make sure you're always prepared for meetings is to take notes or keep in mind what topics are talked about at meetings so you can be prepared to address them during the next meeting. The value you bring to the meetings confirms that everybody is on the same page and helps everybody understand what they need to do to stay there.

Chapter 9

What Will People Say About You When You Leave the Company?

Most people don't want to admit this, but everybody cares about what others think about them. The main people who take the time to sign on to social media to let the world know they don't care what people think about them have actually been offended by what somebody has said about them. Your earliest actions at your job will affect how people perceive you. The moment you arrive for your first day on the job, people will begin to assess you and your capabilities quickly. People will observe you to figure out the answer to these questions:

- Do you have what it takes to make tough decisions?
- Do you have the values I relate to, admire, and want to emulate?
- Are you enthusiastic about the opportunity to make a difference?
- Do you demand high-level performance from others?
- Will you work hard like I do?

Being prepared to answer these questions through your actions will put you in position to make a smooth transition from college to corporate or your career. My manager gave me some advice I will never forget. He told me to pay special attention to the perception I create because other people's perception of me is their reality. He also mentioned that people remember the good and bad about you, but the bad often attaches to people like the person who walks out of a public bathroom with tissue stuck to the bottom of their shoe. Like the tissue, everybody will know about the bad reputation that follows you, even when you want people to just forget it. Working hard and being a team player is a sure way to avoid earning a bad reputation.

Please take this advice from a person who knows how it feels to be viewed by their colleagues as having a shaky reputation for not performing up to the company's standards. This was a challenging experience, but it showed me the importance of gaining your peers' respect. My colleagues didn't understand or care that I was struggling to adjust from college, feeling homesick from being 17 hours away from my family, or adjusting to being a first-time father and husband. They just needed me to do my part and perform. Although I don't believe my corporate colleagues thought I was a bad employee, I do believe they could tell by my actions and lack of production that I wasn't fully interested in being the best employee I could be. The reputation you created for yourself at your previous job or during college can follow you to your next job.

It's important to value your reputation because you never know when your new employer will want to check with your old one to find out what type of employee you really are.

How much would it suck for you to be close to getting your dream job only to receive a rejection email because the employer realized you weren't the right person after they did research and spoke with your previous employers or professors? Your life is an open book with years' worth of chapters that have been completed, as well as chapters that consist of blank pages because you haven't reached certain points in your life yet. The beauty of life is that you can turn bad experiences into priceless learning experiences. You can use moments you want to forget to motivate you to never go down that road again. If your behavior from college and previous jobs still haunt you today, don't lose hope. The first step in transforming your reputation is to be a better person today. Show your colleagues you're a team player by insisting on helping with their work once you've completed your own task. Show your manager they didn't make a bad decision to hire you by coming in earlier and staying later. The only way people can predict how you will perform today or in the future is by observing how you performed in the past and today. You can't change how you performed in the past, but you can change how you perform now.

My high school and college years were interesting because there were moments when I knew a lot about my peers even though I never held a conversation with them. If there was a popular girl or boy at your school, you probably knew a lot about them because they either had a reputation people wanted to emulate or didn't like, which made it the daily gossip. High school and college aren't the only places you can walk into a room and everybody knows who you are even though you have no idea who they are. Your reputation will spread like wildfire among your peers and supervisors, regardless of whether it's good or bad.

I remember seeing people make scenes once they realized they wouldn't be with the company anymore because they got a new job. They would do and say things to managers they wanted to say for years, or they gave very little effort to completing tasks because they felt like it was no longer their problem. There are a few reasons why having this mentality isn't good. The obvious reason for not making choices like this is because future employers may reach out to previous ones to find out what you did. Another reason why you shouldn't burn any bridges is because you never know when you'll need to work for that company again. I've seen numerous people walk away from a job and eventually had to come back years later because they needed a job so they could provide for their families.

Never say never concerning what will happen in life. The best way to approach life and job opportunities is to always do your best even when you don't like the job; at the end of the day, your reputation will greatly affect your future opportunities.

Chapter 10

Find Somebody You Admire and Duplicate Their Success by Being a Mentee

I was born and raised in Bertie County where there are no skyscrapers or major companies, which is probably why I felt like a fish out of water when I experienced life in the inner city of Charlotte, North Carolina. A company flew me into town and treated me like royalty by driving me around in nice cars and placing me in a suite in one of the city's best hotels. If you're not familiar with the process of being interviewed and hired by a corporate company, it can intimidate you and cause you to miss out on great opportunities if you get overwhelmed.

A valuable lesson I learned early in my corporate career is that if I want to be successful at my job, I will need to find somebody who was in a position I'd like to be in in the future. I needed to find a mentor, but I didn't know anybody in the company. So, I just observed and reached out to people who I thought could teach me a thing or two about learning how to be professional and successful. It's important to understand that every important well-dressed executive you see walking around the office was once in your shoes. The only thing that separates the CEO of the company from yourself is time and experience.

I think it's important to remember that everything you experience in college and during your career is all part of the process of becoming the successful person you're destined to be. Your supervisor may seem to have it all together now, but the reason why they're so good at what they do is because they failed often when they were in your position. Taking every opportunity to ask them questions and learn from them will ensure your success because you won't want to make the same mistakes they did.

Knowledge Is the New Money
Making the Transition from College to Corporate or Career

When I worked at Sam's Club Headquarters, my colleagues thought I was a little too fearless in approaching people for advice or about being my mentor. One day, I decided to send Rosalind Brewer, who was the president and CEO at the time, an invite to meet with me, and she actually accepted my invitation. After meeting with her, I found out my colleagues didn't like the idea of me meeting with people in high positions because they thought I was brown-nosing and trying to get promotions without earning them. Not only was I hurt by such allegations, but I was also completely confused as to how I was supposed to learn to be a great corporate employee if people frowned upon seeking mentorship from others who've excelled and advanced within the company. After the Vice President of Sales, who was also an alumnus of North Carolina A&T, realized I was frustrated with the criticism I received from meeting with top executives, he assured me that I was actually making the right decisions to seek people who are successful and emulate their success.

Many people believe that success and promotions will come by showing up to work hard every day, but they're clueless to the fact that working hard isn't the only ingredient to being successful in corporate America. There are *dos and don'ts* you'll need to learn that will help you advance in your career, but the only way you'll learn them is if you seek help from a mentor or somebody who has experienced success within the company. You can do as much research as you like to learn about the company's culture, but your mentor can give you insight about it that you never would've learned on your own. Choose any industry, and you'll find a highly successful person who learned how to be successful from somebody else.

Don't get caught in the trap of believing that you have to figure out everything by yourself. LeBron James modeled his game after Michael Jordan. Cam Newton used to play just like Michael

Vick in high school because he admired his talent. Rapper and hip-hop superstar J. Cole tried to rap just like Nas and Jay Z. All these people once studied how to be successful from people who did it before them, and now they're considered the best at what they do. One day you'll be considered the best at what you do, but the only way that will happen is if you learn from whoever is considered the best at what they do.

You Will Receive Help When People See You Are Trying to Help Yourself

Chris Rock is known for starring in classic movies like "New Jack City" and making thousands of people laugh from his unique comedy. Chris Rock has a way of telling the truth about controversial topics through his jokes, which makes people laugh while thinking at the same time. Chris once said that nobody has ever picked him up when he was thumbing for a ride because his car broke down. People would drive past him as if he didn't exist. But something magical happened when he decided to take the matter into his own hands and attempt to fix his car or push it to the nearest gas station. **When people noticed he was trying to help himself, they stopped immediately and assisted him.**

The best advice that was given to me concerning finding a mentor is this: "When the student is ready, the teacher will appear." People are more willing to help you when they notice that you are trying to help yourself. When people within the company see that you're eager to learn and that you're working very hard to excel at your job, they will automatically approach you to show you how to perform more efficiently and effectively. You've also seen this during your collegiate years. The professor didn't go out of their way to help the student who showed up late to class and sat all the way in the back of the classroom; they actually reached out to the student who struggled academically but tried their best to do better. I have found this to be true as an entrepreneur, author, and real estate investor, too. Nobody reached out to me to show me how to start my own company or how to write a book. I just took a leap of faith and approached customers and clients with confidence that my business would satisfy their needs and desires. I picked up my laptop every day and started typing even though I had no idea how to write and publish a book. **When I got to a point where I needed help, people magically came into my life to show me how to get to the next stage.** People gravitated toward me and wanted to help because they saw how passionate I was about being successful at whatever I was trying to do.

I'm qualified to give you this advice because I've also been the guy who put forth very little effort but expected people to help me. The only people who'll be more than happy to assist you while you aren't trying to help yourself are your parents, family, or close friends because they love you and always want to see you do well in life. Unfortunately, this type of treatment will do you more harm than good in your future endeavors. Depending on people to bail you out of situations when you aren't trying to help yourself creates a false perception that society consists of many people who're waiting to help you when you haven't done your part to help yourself. The key to obtaining success and attracting people that will help you attain success is to give 150% in all you do at all times. Successful people have a strong work ethic and very little tolerance for people who are lazy or want something for nothing. The reason why successful people often reach out to assist others when they see them trying is because they remember when somebody took the time to help them when they were trying to figure out life. Successful people can see your ambition and hunger for success in your hard work and drive.

The next time you speak with your professor or manager,

pay close attention to how passionate they are about the advice they give you. Look in their eyes and notice how they take pride in helping you through this process because they remember the days when they needed advice from somebody. Quit waiting for somebody to come and save you because life is hard. Stop waiting for people to feel sorry for you because it's taking longer to achieve your goals than you expected. The sooner you brush yourself off and continue to work hard to make your dreams a reality, the sooner you'll attract other successful people who want you to join their team, company, or movement.

Chapter 11

Unrealistic Dreams Are the Key to Success

Having unrealistic dreams is how I went from growing up in poverty to flying around in a private corporate jet. Unrealistic dreams played a huge role in me graduating from college, even though I struggled early on during the first two years. Unrealistic dreams are the reason why I eventually worked at Sam's Club Headquarters even though I didn't attend a top graduate program or have a highly impressive GPA. Unrealistic dreams are the reason why I'm the first author, entrepreneur, and real estate investor in my family. There's no way that some of the greats would have achieved such success if they were realistic about their situation and what statistics said they could achieve. Being realistic about your situation may prevent you from striving to work for a company in a different state because nobody in your family has ever left the state for work. Or maybe you've never been an A student, which means the odds are against you becoming one. Unless you think unrealistically and believe you can become an A student, you'll never realize that dream.

Every person who's achieved an abundance of success had to believe they could be successful even when their current situation didn't look promising. If you try to be realistic about your situation, you'll just accept what people say you should have or will be in your life. Yes, it may be true that nobody in your family has ever enrolled in and graduated from college and it's considered unrealistic for you to dream you can do so, but it's the only way you can live your dream. You have to believe you can do something you've never done before to achieve massive levels of success you've never achieved before.

Les Brown once said, "Making a million dollars is easy, but

believing you can make a million dollars is challenging." If he didn't have the unrealistic dream of becoming a millionaire, he would've never been brave enough to pursue his dreams. The Wright brothers had unrealistic dreams of creating a vehicle that would be capable of flying to different locations through the air. People told them they were delusional and unrealistic, but they persevered through the doubt and created the airplanes we benefit from today.

Take a moment to ask yourself if you have realistic dreams and expectations or if you're brave enough to dream further than what your circumstances look like. Your answer will determine how successful you'll become in the future.

Unrealistic Dreams + Realistic Work Ethic = Success

Being unrealistic about life can cause you more discomfort, hard times, and failure than you'd like. One of the challenges I endured with having unrealistic dreams is that people would tell me that I was irresponsible or delusional. I eventually realized I deserved the criticism I was getting because I forgot to include the realistic work ethic that would be needed to become successful. After I read a book called "The 10X Rule" by Grant Cardone, I realized your dreams and goals should be bigger than what they are, but your work ethic and effort to achieve your goals should be more than what they are, as well. The problem with most people and the reason why young adults struggle to obtain success is that they either work extremely hard to achieve average goals or they set ambitious unrealistic goals but aren't realistic about the work ethic it will take to achieve them. It's not good enough to just be a dreamer and have unrealistic goals. You have to be willing to work harder than what you think it will take to achieve them. Your ambitious unrealistic dreams have to be matched by your realistic work ethic.

Most college students have friends in their hometown that

decided not to attend college for whatever reason. They may believe their friends' aspirations of graduating and becoming a lawyer are unrealistic because they don't have the same drive, ambition, or dream. You'll notice that people will try to put a limit on your abilities simply because they can't see themselves being as successful as you aspire to be. They'll tell you to "get real" when you tell them about your plans to attend one of the top colleges in America. I'll never forget the day when I was speaking with my cousin about someday working at the headquarters of a major company. We were both attending historically black colleges at the moment, which I was very proud of. He looked at me and said, "It's impossible to graduate from a historically black college and get hired to work at a big-time company." After we took turns going back and forth about who was wrong and who was right, I realized there was a bigger issue at hand. I realized his mind wouldn't allow him to dream past Bertie County and his current situation, but my mind took me to different places and cultures all over the world. His imagination took him as far as his eyes could see, but mine looked past what statistics said I could or couldn't do. I always believed that if something could be done, I could do it. Years later when I was working at Sam's Club Headquarters, I could only think about where I would be if I pursued safe, realistic dreams rather than the ambitious, unrealistic dream I was currently living. Don't allow the fear of failure to be the reason why you choose a safe path in life versus one that will allow you to live your dream. You'll experience failure regardless of the path you take, so you may as well pursue the path that will be maximized by your passion and purpose.

  Somebody once asked Beyonce during an interview, "What does fear taste like?" She responded, "Fear tastes like success." She explained that when you walk into fear, you walk into faith. As you pursue the next step in your life's journey, you have to make sure you don't run away from opportunities because you fear you'll fail or experience uncomfortable moments. Dealing with fear is the toll you have to pay in order to someday live your dream; it's part of the process. ***It's okay to be fearful at times, but it's not okay to allow that fear to stop you from being the best version of you.*** As an entrepreneur and a real estate investor, I face fear more often than not, but I keep moving forward because I understand that the only reason why I'm fearful at times is because I've never done what I'm attempting to do.

Chapter 12

A Sense of Entitlement Is a Cancerous Mentality to Have

One day, I was talking to my dad, and he was telling me about how he felt robbed because he believed he was next in line for a promotion that was given to someone who didn't have as much tenure as he had. He believed seniority alone qualified him to have a promotion or new position handed to him. I used to have a mentality like my dad and hundreds of thousands of people around the world who believe they deserve to have something given to them, regardless of whether they earned it or not. I thought as long as I showed up for class or work, I should be rewarded like everybody else. Parents, teachers, and society have given youth the idea that they'll be rewarded as long as they just show up. Getting promotions or recognition based on tenure and just showing up may have been the way to advance in the past, but today this type of mentality will cause you to be overlooked, underpaid, and unappreciated.

Working in corporate America taught me an invaluable lesson about how you have to do more than show up to be considered successful; you have to bring something to the table to prove to your manager that you're ready for the next level in life. Many college graduates walk into their career with a sense of entitlement. They believe they should get a certain salary and be treated a certain way because of where they went to school, who their parents are, what their parents achieved, or what they accomplished in the past. It took me a while to realize that the main reason why I struggled in corporate America is because I thought I was entitled to more money even though I knew I probably wouldn't be ready to handle the workload that would be expected from me at that level.

Knowledge Is the New Money
Making the Transition from College to Corporate or Career

A sense of entitlement is a horrible mindset to have because it creates the perception that you're lazy and that you believe good grades and thousands of dollars should just be thrown at you for unrealistic reasons. An entitled mindset could be the result of having things handed to you all your life, or it can be the result of having a rough upbringing, which makes you refuse to settle for anything less than your standards or expectations. Having high expectations while being willing to work hard will put you in position to enjoy much success, but high expectations without being willing to work hard is a recipe for failure. Realizing my dad had a sense of entitlement concerning his job helped me understand that anybody at any age can fall into the trap of feeling like they deserved something regardless of if they actually earned it. The quickest way to get on your colleagues and boss's bad side is to expect something for nothing. Whether you deserve the promotion or not, you immediately take the power out of your hands when you don't follow your high expectations with hard work and determination. Anything that's worth having in life takes hard work, consistency, and faith to acquire. You don't get in life what you want; you get what you produce or earn.

You can use this philosophy or approach to every situation in life. Say your family loves cake, but they mostly love the middle section because it has the perfect amount of texture and moisture. If you don't hurry and get to the kitchen in time, your siblings will eat the best part of the cake and leave you with the outside pieces. You showed up just like your siblings did to eat a slice of cake, but they put forth more effort to make it to the kitchen quickly, which resulted in them earning the best part of the cake and you receiving the part that was picked over and not wanted.

Let's think about this approach with a different example you can probably relate to better. Everybody has experienced either the humbling feeling of being chosen last for a game of basketball or the proud feeling of being picked first. The person who is picked first has usually done something to warrant being chosen first. They have some type of specialty or skill set that will give the team a competitive advantage and help them win the game. At some point in time, the person who was chosen last created the perception that they don't specialize in anything or just aren't very good at playing basketball. They may show up to the basketball court every day, but their work ethic and skill set is average at best. The person isn't average; their mentality and desire to work hard is. Regardless of the sport, industry, or field, you'll find that the people who earn success will receive the opportunity to be chosen first and the people who feel entitled but aren't willing to grind and put in the necessary work will receive other people's crumbs, hand-me-downs, and second-tier opportunities. Do not allow an entitled mentality to kill your momentum—give your all in everything you do.

Chapter 13
Your Goals & Actions Are too Small

We've never met, but I know something about you that will blow your mind. I know you have dreams and aspirations of being successful in life. You want to graduate from college so your parents will be proud of you. You want to eventually make a lot of money so you can provide for your family and buy the things you always desired. You want to stop procrastinating so you can make better grades, lose weight, or finally update your resume and apply for jobs. I also know you don't want to be a failure. I know that the goals you've set for yourself up until this point in your life have been too small, and the actions you're taking to achieve them aren't enough.

Ask yourself one question: "Do I set goals compared to what others have achieved and what their goals are, or do I set goals that are congruent with maximizing my potential?" You could set a goal to make the same amount of money your peers make after college, but you could be putting a limit on how much you could make by doing so. Your peers' salary may be around $40,000-$60,000, and they may remain in that range for years. If you set goals similar to your peers, you will achieve similar goals. But what would happen if you were to set a goal to make six figures a year within five years of graduating college? If you set bigger goals, you will put yourself in position to accomplish more than you would have if you didn't set them to begin with. You have what it takes to be the first millionaire in your family, but if you set goals that are too small, you'll make the same amount of money as your peers. You have what it takes to earn many promotions at your new job within a short period of time, but you are content with your current position because you notice most people your age remain in their position for years before they get a promotion. If you don't challenge yourself to do and have more in life, you'll settle for what your peers, friends, and family have settled for because you'll think it's normal.

Why do you think LeBron James has the opportunity to showcase his talent in the NBA but there's a guy who is just as talented working a 9-to-5 job somewhere? How come Gabrielle Union can demand millions of dollars to act in a movie, but the young lady who's extremely talented and attends your church only showcases her gift during the Christmas plays? The difference between the presidents of the United States and those who have just been class presidents is their goals and willingness to work hard to achieve their goals.

Isn't it exciting to know that the only difference between greatness and mediocrity is what you expect to acquire in life and the mindset to make it happen? I don't know about you, but the last sentence gets me pumped up every time I read it. If I didn't set big goals for myself, I would not be an author, and you would not be reading this book today. I would be just another person who loves to read and someone who's experienced many trials and tribulations in life but is too afraid to transform my story into a blueprint to help change people's lives.

What does dreaming big and working hard to make your dream become a reality have to do with transitioning from college to corporate or your career? Everything! This shift in mindset will be the major key to experiencing a plethora of success in corporate America.

What Goals Would You Set If You Knew You Wouldn't Fail?

If you ever wonder if you're living up to your full potential, just ask yourself one question: "If failure wasn't an option, what goals would I pursue?" Wherever your mind takes you while you think about the answer, there lies the path to what you should pursue in life. The worst feeling in life is not when you fail; it's when you pass up an opportunity to succeed because you were too afraid you'd fail. Your success in college and life afterward depends on your ability to understand that although you could come up short of the goal you set, each failure is actually a setup for a comeback.

Often times, we may think we're losing at the game of life when we're actually winning. Don't be afraid to apply for a job opportunity at that large corporation because you're afraid you won't have what it takes to be an asset to the company. If you fear you don't have what it takes to bring value to a company, become the person you desire to be. Become the type of employee who will add value to the company and industry you desire to work in. There's this perception that most people have life all figured out. The truth is that most people are afraid and unsure about themselves. Regardless of whether they graduated at the top of their class or just barely graduated, everybody worries about not being as good as advertised once they're hired. The best way to overcome this fear is to face it head on. **Work on your weaknesses and build on your strengths.**

It's been said that most people fail at accomplishing their goals before they even start because they don't have the appropriate mindset needed to live their dreams. Muhammad Ali, Mike Tyson, and Floyd Mayweather all had the same effect on their opponents. Their opponents lost the fight before they stepped in the boxing ring because they never believed they actually had a realistic chance of beating the greats. The reason why Buster Douglas beat Mike Tyson is because he actually believed he would beat him. Buster understood that Tyson was a great fighter, so he realized the only way he could beat him is if he worked on his weaknesses and improved his strengths. Buster promised his mom before she died that he would beat Mike Tyson, which indicates he believed he could do what nobody else in the world believed he could.

Pay close attention to your mindset because it impacts the decisions you make and the results you produce. Applying to that job, seeking a promotion, applying to the college of your dreams, applying for internships, and traveling to a different state to interview for a job all require an amount of faith that's past the average person's understanding. Everybody says they have positive mindsets and that they're faith-oriented until they have to really put their faith to the test. I found that successful people have three attributes that set them apart from average and below-average people. The first is that they do what unsuccessful people don't want to do. Many people would prefer to sit on their couch and eat potato chips instead of working out, but the people who are healthy and fit get up and work out, regardless of how they feel. It's been said that public speaking is the #1 fear in the world and that death is ranked #2. People actually fear speaking in public more than they fear dying! Although this statistic may be true, it doesn't stop comedians such as Kevin Hart from getting on stage in front of thousands of people to tell jokes. You may say, "Well, that's easy for him to do because he's been doing it for a while." Yes, he has been entertaining the world for a while, but at some point, he had to take a leap of faith and do what the average person is afraid to do. I was speaking with a friend a few months ago, and he told me he always wanted to be a comedian but was too shy and afraid to stand up in front of people. I was completely shocked when he told me this because based on the path he settled for in life, I would've never guessed he aspired to be a comedian. Fear of failure resulted in him living a life that was totally different than what he wanted or expected.

The second attribute that differentiates successful from average people is that they understand the importance of being self-disciplined. Self-discipline is where most people fall short, and it's the reason why few achieve success that others dream of. Many people talk about what they will do, few people will start doing what they said they will do, and even fewer will be consistent until they see their plan through and produce results. Only the successful people will start and finish what they said they would do. Being disciplined is the ultimate equalizer in life because it will allow you to achieve as much or more than you can imagine through sacrifice and commitment. Nobody can stop you from losing weight as long as you are disciplined enough to create healthier lifestyle habits. Your friends cannot affect your GPA as long as you are disciplined enough to study on a consistent basis, even when they're out partying. Your colleagues can't stop you from getting a promotion as long as you're reaching and hitting the goals and metrics that were set by your boss or manager. When you set your mind to get a promotion at your job, you will be disciplined enough to do what it takes to qualify for the next role and remind management consistently through your words and actions that you're the right person for the upcoming promotion.

  The third attribute that separates the successful from the unsuccessful is uncommon faith. Rather than having ordinary faith like most people, they have extraordinary faith. I'm a man of faith not only because that's how I was raised, but, most importantly, it's also how I experienced such success at a young age even though I came from humble beginnings. I believe many guys from my hometown in Bertie County wanted to write a book on a topic that was interesting to them, but for some reason, they didn't pursue that path. You don't hear often about guys from my hometown going on to work at the headquarters for some of the largest companies in the world. I didn't grow up with a family full of entrepreneurs who would allow me to believe I could repeat their success. The only way I could become an author and entrepreneur is if I had uncommon faith. I'm a firm believer that we get out of life what we ask of it; the problem is that we often ask for average stuff. Instead of praying and asking for the ability to graduate with a great GPA and obtain a job to make more money than your family ever made so you can provide for your loved ones, you pray to just make it to graduation because you're tired of being in school. Joel Osteen said it best in his book "Break Out!" He said, "I've learned that when you have uncommon faith, you will see uncommon results." The people who're praised for being so brave, talented, and successful are often put on a pedestal for doing something anybody can do. The only difference between them and the people who are praising them is that they believe differently.

Although you may not have people in your family who've made a smooth transition from college to corporate America or their career, you'll be the first to do so if you have uncommon faith. By having a faith that's different from the people you've been around your entire life, you will live a life and experience success that average people won't. People will look at you and wonder what's different about you, and they'll be oblivious to the fact that you simply just made up your mind to operate in unshakeable, uncommon faith and detach yourself from common, mediocre faith. My life changed when I stopped asking God to help me provide for my family and started asking him to put me in a position to provide for my kids, grandkids, and strangers all over the world.

Believe in the impossible and watch it become possible.

Chapter 14

Shameless Persistence
Propels You from Good to Great

At some point in your life, you've been trained to believe that good is enough. Getting a pat on the back while being told "good job" has always been confirmation that your effort was just good enough to get by. But how will you respond when you someday realize that level of effort is suddenly not good enough?

I had a friend who was extremely smart and always made good grades in high school. I used to think he was from a different planet because I couldn't understand how he never made a B, whereas I considered myself lucky if I could at least make a C at times. I would've never thought in a million years that I would've been the one to graduate from college and he'd drop out. College was the first time he actually had to study to make a good grade. The effort he put forth his entire life suddenly wasn't good enough. It was hard for him to understand the importance of persevering to achieve a goal because he never had to do that before. The only reason I graduated from college is because I embraced the fact that I had to be persistent to earn my degree.

I'd be lying if I told you I never wanted to quit. I had to be persistent to get the opportunity to work at the headquarters of Sam's Club and Belk because companies looked at my GPA and instantly thought not to hire me. I was persistent with emailing and calling recruiters. I was persistent with searching and applying for jobs. I found out eventually that being persistent in your endeavors plays a bigger role in determining your future than using your God-given talents to obtain success.

When I first made the decision to invest in real estate, it was very challenging because I didn't have much money to play with, and to make matters worse, I had a family to support. Being persistent played a major role in me eventually making more money in a month than what I made in a year before I went in business for myself. Although I lacked capital and didn't know all the right people to help me get my business off the ground, I was very persistent in following through with small productive habits every day. Once I realized I couldn't afford to send postcards and mail to potential motivated home sellers, I began to cold call them, which allowed me to build rapport and relationships with them. Even when people told me they weren't ready to sell their house, I would call them the next month and the month after until they were.

It's been said that luck is when preparation meets opportunities. I seriously believe that being persistent should be included in that equation because successful people all over the world will tell you that they wouldn't be where they are today if they gave up when they heard "no" for the first, second, or third time. You remember those times when you kept asking your parents for money or the chance to go to a party and continued to ask them until they finally said "yes"? You wanted to go to that party so badly that you weren't bothered by the *"nos."* You realized that every "no" was one step closer to that one "yes" you wanted.

The funny part about being persistent is that sometimes you'll get your way simply because people will get tired of telling you "no." Being persistent about making good grades in school, applying for that job, and attempting to date your high school or college sweetheart will eventually pay off. I often smile when I look at my wife because I still remember how she rejected me when I first tried to date her during my freshman year of college. She stood me up, wouldn't return my calls, and sometimes seemed to be interested in other guys, but I remained persistent to let her know I was serious about wanting to date her. Fifteen years later I still think about how being persistent is the ultimate reason why the young lady who once gave me the cold shoulder is now my wife and the mother of my children.

Persistency and Laziness Cannot Coexist

The only way persistency and laziness can exist at the same time is if you are persistent at being lazy. My 2-year-old son is very determined to do what he wants to do. I'm ashamed to admit that there have been moments when I said "yes" to giving my son a cookie or watching his favorite cartoon simply because I was tired of saying "no." His desire to get what he wanted inspired him to keep going until he eventually got it. However, the energy and persistency from him is completely different when it comes to doing something he doesn't want to do. One night, I asked him to walk to the kitchen and put his bottle in the refrigerator, but to my surprise, he looked at me and said, "Michael tired." My son could be persistent when it came to doing something he really wanted to do, but he showed no sign of being persistent when he was being lazy and didn't want to do something. If this trait exists in a 2-year-old, I can only imagine the hard work it will take to resist being lazy and be persistent in pursuing your dreams and aspirations for the rest of your life.

From the moment you walk on your college campus to the moment you get hired at your first job post-graduation, you'll always face moments when you can be persistent and see something through to the end or take the easy way out. I actually believe it's human nature to gravitate towards being lazy, but that doesn't make it right. The people you've watched make good grades and seem to always get promotions aren't successful because they're extremely smart. Believing people are successful because they're smart is a lazy way to analyze and figure out why you keep hitting singles while other people appear to be hitting home runs consistently.

Knowledge Is the New Money
Making the Transition from College to Corporate or Career

Successful people live the life they desire because they fight the urge to be lazy, realizing that will only lead them down the bitter path to mediocrity. Being persistent is the key to living your dream. This one word can change your life and allow you to attain all the success you desire, but it's the reason why most people remain in the average club rather than enjoying life in the persistence club.

It doesn't take any effort to be lazy. Laziness doesn't discriminate because it will attack both a homeless person on the street who believes their life is not worth living and some of the wealthiest people in the world who feel like they have everything they could ever want. A single mom or dad of five kids faces the same level of temptation to be lazy as the single, childless 20-year-old with no obligations. Laziness and procrastination have caused many people to live a life below what they're capable of while other people have overcome laziness by persistently striving to achieve their goals. If you don't have some type of motivation as to why you should fight the urge to be lazy, you'll be like a defeated boxer in the ring staggering one punch away from a TKO and watching their dreams fade away right before their eyes. You'll be lying flat on the canvas while the winner, *laziness,* is raising its hands in the air with the championship belt around its waist once again. Laziness may have defeated your family, friends, or even you in the past, but it doesn't have to defeat you from today forward.

A pretty cool trick I use to fight the urge to be lazy is to think about how much it'll hurt me if I enjoy a moment of laziness rather than getting closer to accomplishing a goal. You can gossip and have fun during your 30-minute lunch break at work, or you can use those precious moments to study for an upcoming exam. You can spend the majority of your time complaining about what you don't like about your job like the rest of your colleagues, or you can find ways to continuously set yourself apart by improving your skills to attract a promotion from your current or an external company. Laziness invites everybody to the party, but only the driven, focused people will turn down the invitation because they prefer to plan for a brighter future.

I was often looked at as an outcast when I worked in retail during college because I preferred to spend every second of my spare time doing something productive that would create the life I wanted to live in the future. The reason why I skipped over many operations' manager positions at Walmart stores to work at the headquarters is because I continued to grind during my free time while everybody else preferred to chill. Nobody seemed to be satisfied with their current situation, but they weren't willing to fight the urge to be lazy for the sake of investing in themselves for a bright future. Don't let that be you.

Chapter 15

You Have Everything You Need to Get Anything You Want

Daymond John, the star of "Shark Tank," wrote a book called "The Power of Broke." I was excited to purchase and read this book because I had a feeling it would confirm what I already believed about achieving more while having few resources. As crazy as it may sound, you're actually being prepared for greatness when you're forced to create results with few resources. You want those new shoes, but you don't have enough money to buy them. You need more time to work on your dream business, but there doesn't seem to be enough time in the day. You want to learn how to produce music and make beats, but you don't have the money or the right person to teach you the ropes. You want to create better results at your company, but you believe you need more help in your department to make that happen. The average person quits at the first sign of adversity. I like to look at adversity as being a club bouncer. Once the bouncer views your ID and realizes you're qualified to enter the building, you can walk in freely. Adversity is no different. Adversity stops you at the doorstep of your dreams just to make sure you want to be as successful as you say you do. People who give up on their dreams don't realize they're qualified to live them, so they give up at the first sign of adversity or hardship. You may not be as smart as the person who graduated at the top of your class, but you have the willpower to out-study and out-work them. You may not have the internship experiences and high GPAs like other students, but you arrive earlier and stay longer at your job until you master the information. You can't control the lifestyle your parents created for you, but you can control the effort you put into creating a brighter tomorrow.

Excitement should shoot through your body like a bolt of

lightning when you realize you already have what you need to get anything you want. Anything you don't have, you'll eventually get through failure, learning experiences, and adversity. Real success is when you can experience failure many times without losing enthusiasm. A few years ago, Steve Harvey made one of the biggest mistakes of his career. While announcing the new Miss America, he crowned the wrong person. Instead of crowning Miss Philippines, he crowned Miss Columbia. Not only was this an embarrassing moment for the contestants, it was, obviously one for Steve, too. He was already famous, wealthy, and successful before this embarrassing moment, but this was actually a moment of personal and professional growth for him. It gave him the type of humility you can get only through adversity. He made the world laugh for years while he told his jokes as a comedian, but now the world had the opportunity to watch him ask for forgiveness. Steve thought he had everything success could give him, but he learned he could always receive more by experiencing hardships, embarrassment, and adversity.

As intimidating as college and your first job will be, don't underestimate your ability to succeed. You have everything you need to be a successful college student and professional in corporate America. If you feel like you're not as smart as other college students, study longer and harder. If you feel like a fish out of water in corporate America because nobody in your family has ever been there before, observe the culture and adapt to it so that you'll fit in and eventually stand out in the best way possible.

"Why Do I Need College and Corporate America if I Want to Be an Entrepreneur?"

I always wondered why I needed to go to college or get a corporate job since my ultimate goal was to go into business for myself. This mindset played a role in why I struggled in college and in corporate America since I had a hard time understanding how my desire to work for myself had anything to do with either of those. Like many youth and young adults, I never liked doing busy work or doing something I believed wasn't getting me closer to achieving my goals. However, I didn't realize that every task I had to do gave me the chance to hone skills I would later need and use in the future. Remember, you have everything you need to get anything you want, but you will continue to get what you need through adversity, embarrassing moments, and difficult times.

 College and corporate America are great environments to mature and prepare you for entrepreneurship. My first corporate job gave me the task of managing $250 million worth of inventory. The experience I got from managing millions of dollars was worth more than my salary. They didn't care about me being inexperienced since I never had a corporate job before. The expectations they had for me broke me down and stripped away all the qualities that would make me a weak, irresponsible entrepreneur.

 I have to be honest with you: college and corporate America gave me some of the worst and best experiences I've ever had. They turned my weaknesses into strengths and my strengths into competitive advantages. I went into college as a shy young man with big dreams, but it transformed me to become a guy with big dreams who was capable of expressing and communicating effectively. So, let me encourage you not to take college or your job for granted because you don't think you'll be there for a long time or because you'd prefer to start your own company. Take this opportunity to figure out how you can learn something that could not only take your current company to another level, but that will also improve your future company. What if your reputation from college or your job could lead to opportunities as an entrepreneur? Often times, it's who you know not what you know. The people you'll meet in college and at your job can become future clients or business partners once you start your own company. You never know who is watching you or who would invest money or time in your future company. You may look at the person who sits beside you as just a colleague, but they could someday be your business partner if they're impressed with your work ethic and how you carry yourself at your job.

I was asked a very good question concerning why I chose to write a book about transitioning from college to corporate America or your career since I've stated before that I believe the best way to attain wealth is going into business for yourself. I'm advocating for youth and young adults to attend college and work in corporate America before they attempt to go in business for themselves because they'll learn from their mistakes in a less painful way than if they immediately started as an entrepreneur. I was terrible at paying attention to details and being persistent in achieving my goals when I first graduated from college. I would hate to see how much money I would've lost and the reputation I would've received if I went in business for myself straight out of college or without even going to college. Of course, there are some exceptions to the rule. Bill Gates and Mark Zuckerburg both dropped out of college to pursue their dreams of creating Microsoft and Facebook. Unfortunately, most people aren't Bill Gates or Mark Zuckerburg. Mark Cuban, a serial investor and entrepreneur, understood that dropping out of college to pursue his dream could hurt him in the long run, so he graduated from college and worked for a company for a little while before starting on his own. Mark was able to use the networking skills he learned in college and the knowledge of building a company from corporate America to inspire him to go into business for himself.

So, if you need any motivation to stay in school or get a corporate job, just remember you could learn one thing from both that could be the difference between you going out of business as an entrepreneur after three years or making millions of dollars from building an empire that will be beneficial for generations to come. Many people who eventually become an entrepreneur never thought they'd become one. I've heard people become entrepreneurs because they got laid off and I've also heard of people who started a business because they wanted to control their own destiny. The reason why most people including myself become entrepreneurs is because they desired freedom. You may feel trapped by college and your corporate job now but take all the lessons you learn in those environments—plus the ones you've learned in this book—to become a better version of yourself and **MAKE YOUR DREAMS COME TRUE.**

www.ingramcontent.com/pod-product-compliance
Lightning Source LLC
LaVergne TN
LVHW051151080426
835508LV00021B/2573